Sight-Reading
Made Easy

WRITTEN BY TOM FLEMING

Amsco Publications
A Part of The **Music Sales Group**
New York/London/Paris/Sydney/Copenhagen/Berlin/Tokyo/Madrid

Cover photography by Peter Svarzbein, assisted by Greg Wilson
Models: Ethan Campbell, Canyon, Sonia De Los Santos,
Megan Leach, and Akil (Myself) Omari
Cover design by Josh Labouve

CD credits:
All guitars: Tom Fleming
Bass: Neil Williams
Drums: Brett Morgan
Recorded & mixed by Jonas Persson and John Rose

Project editor: David Bradley
Interior design and layout by Len Vogler

*Thanks to Heather Ramage for her understanding and patience,
and to Rick Cardinali for all the tea and cakes.*

Order No. AM 982333
International Standard Book Number: 0.8256.3456.3

Exclusive Distributors:
Music Sales Corporation
257 Park Avenue South, New York, NY 10010 USA
Music Sales Limited
8/9 Frith Street, London W1D 3JB England
Music Sales Pty. Limited
120 Rothschild Street, Rosebery, Sydney, NSW 2018, Australia

Printed in the United States of America by
Vicks Lithograph and Printing Corporation

Table of Contents

CD track listing

This book is all about improving your sight-reading skills using "real-world" examples—the types of guitar parts you will actually encounter in all sorts of situations, from wedding bands to film sessions, should you be lucky enough...

There are many books of sight-reading studies on the market, or rather many books *claiming* to contain sight-reading studies. The trouble is, most of them are actually scale/arpeggio studies:

etc...

While this sort of thing is very useful in terms of getting to know the fretboard, is it useful sight-reading practice? Well, no. It bears absolutely no resemblance to anything you will encounter in a gig or session setting. It doesn't even look the same, because the charts you will see will most likely be written by hand. (The notation in this book simulates the hand-written style you will most often encounter "on the job.") In a nutshell, it's not a piece of music.

The trouble with *real* guitar music, on the other hand, is that it's such an enormously varied mess of different musical styles and different types of notation (dots, chord charts, rhythm slashes, etc.) that it's very difficult to devise any kind of structured approach to learning to read it.

Many guitarists can read music to a basic level, but lack the confidence and stamina to translate the dots on the page into a convincing performance. Why is this? I believe it's because classical musicians spend years playing in orchestras; in this situation, stopping the rest of the orchestra so you can

figure out a particular phrase is not an option, so you just have to get on with it. Most guitarists (and pop/rock musicians in general) miss out on this type of experience. Sitting at home trying to learn to read from books of scale studies, as well as being rather boring, just doesn't instill this type of stamina: every time you stop to work something out, your confidence suffers and a pattern of negative thought is established.

I learned to read properly at music college, sitting head to head with an inspirational teacher, playing *real music*. We'd read it together, but no matter what I played, what mistakes I made, he didn't stop. I would mess up a note, phrase, or a whole line, but he'd still be playing. I would figure out where he was and decide where to come back in. With time, these gaps got shorter and shorter.

This book aims to replicate this orchestral/teacher-driven experience. What ever you do, the CD won't stop for you. And whatever you do, don't stop the CD in the middle of a piece.

How to use this book

Do not attempt to learn the pieces in this book. Trying to memorize them, or spending more time on each of them than allowed by the following rules will compromise the objective, which is to develop real-world sight-reading skills, along with the confidence and stamina to put those skills into practice.

The "pieces" in this book are generally twelve to sixteen measures long, and are as stylistically varied as possible. Another variable is in the type of notation used: some are lead parts (notated in "dots"), some are rhythm parts notated as chord charts (with or without precise rhythms), and some are a combination of the two.

Each piece corresponds to one CD track. The first part of the track is a backing track; the tune is then repeated immediately with the written guitar part present in the mix.

Here's how it works:

1. Choose a piece to attempt, either at random or by going through the book in order; the pieces have been "randomized" in any case.

2. Allow thirty seconds to look through the chart. Note the style, tempo, key, the type of written part, the required sound, and any other relevant information. Select an appropriate sound.

3. Press play. After a count-in, make the best attempt you can to play the written part along with the backing track. To get the most out of this process, resist the temptation to "coast" through it, or to listen to the backing track first and then re-start the track. Play as if it *really matters*. Imagine that you are auditioning for a job and it's all riding on getting this one tune right!

4. After the end of the tune, the count-in starts again immediately, within the same CD track. This time the demonstration guitar part is present. This is your opportunity to check how well you performed. Did you get the right idea? Did you play the written notes, chords and rhythms accurately? In many cases, it's not a simple question of right and wrong, particularly where the part is a chord chart or a simple riff, with instructions such as "ad lib." or "cont. sim." (see *Notation Guide* on page 8). There is a great deal of room for interpretation—it's more a case of me, your teacher, saying, "Here's how I did it."

Most players, even advanced readers, will find some of the pieces in this book very challenging. Some of them, on the other hand, are very easy. This mirrors the experience of sight-reading (or, indeed, of being a musician in general) in the real world. Don't be disheartened if you make a mess of a given piece—you will learn from the experience. I'll say it again: Do not try to learn the piece in order to be able to play it perfectly with the backing track—this defeats the purpose. You will gain more from the experience if you carry on and try another piece. Having played all of them, there is no way you will remember much about many of them, so you can go through the book again, getting as much benefit from it as the first time.

The golden rule of learning to sight-read: **DON'T STOP!** This may seem obvious, and is of course the reason why playing with a teacher, or along with the backing tracks such as those found on the CD, is of much greater value than playing unaccompanied study pieces. The most important skill to develop is playing with confidence; play something that *works*, with confidence and style, and your audience will be impressed and happy. Of course, the ultimate goal is to play the written part accurately, too—if a composer has written a specific melody or rhythm, that's what he wants to hear—but it is better to play something musical, something that works within the given context, than to play the written notes accurately, but sounding *as though you are reading them for the first time*.

At the end of the CD track, hit "pause" and ask yourself, honestly, how well you performed. Most of the time, you will not have played *exactly* what I played. All of the charts leave some room for interpretation (some leave a great deal), and my performance is just that: a performance.

Most of the lead parts are fairly non-specific about details such as bends, hammer-ons, pull-offs, slides, and the like. This is quite deliberate. Most real-world guitar parts don't include this type of information. It's up to you, the player, to turn the part in front of you (which, ultimately is just some black shapes on a white page) into music. For this reason, you may well find that you used a bend in a particular place where I used a slide, or vice versa. The important points are:

1. Did you *understand* the part? This is the most important thing when sight-reading under pressure. Take a quick look and say to yourself, *Ah yes, chugging power chords* [or palm-muted reggae/rock'n'roll rhythm/screaming lead/floaty chords...]. *Yes, I can do that.*

2. Did your performance work with the backing track to produce a satisfactory musical result?

3. Did you play any real "howlers"? We all do it from time to time; this comes back to understanding the part as much as playing the notes accurately. If you have grasped the style and key fully, you are less likely to play a horren-dously wrong note or chord than if you are simply "winging it" from one bar to the next.

4. As I've said, the demonstration mix (with guitar present) is a point of reference rather than an exact transcription. On the other hand, it's worth listening to attentively and learning from it. This is not to say that my playing is perfect either; where there is room for interpretation and ad libs, you may think, *Hey, that's cool, I might do that next time I'm playing something like this...*or you may find my playing tasteless and inappropriate. The point is that you can learn from it either way.

If, and only if, you feel that you failed to grasp the essentials of the part completely, and played nothing of any merit on your first attempt, but understand it perfectly now after hearing the demonstration, you may have one more go. After all, this would happen in a rehearsal situation. Stop the CD after the first part (don't listen to the demonstration again) and compare your two attempts.

Good luck, and remember to enjoy it!

The type of notation used in this book corresponds, in general terms, to the notation found on parts written by real-world arrangers writing for wedding bands, big bands, film sessions and so on, rather than published guitar music. If you are unfamiliar with some aspects of this, the following pages will tell you everything you need to know.

First, the blindingly obvious fact: there is no TAB! That's right, no crutches. This is the main difference between most published guitar music and real guitar parts. Though the pieces in this book are short enough to fit on a single page even with TAB, many real charts run to at least three pages even without it; six pages would simply be too unwieldy on a music stand. In any case, there simply isn't time in many situations to absorb the information on the TAB staff. This does mean, of course, that there is some freedom of choice in where to play any given note or notes—ultimately, it's a musical decision left to the individual player.

There is a lot of important information contained at the very beginning of the chart:

Style. This is a broad indicator, and is meant to be generally helpful. Styles in this book include rock, pop, blues, disco, and funk.

Tempo. Another useful indicator, but don't check it with a metronome before starting the CD. Try to develop an inner sense of tempo.

Key and time signatures. The two most important pieces of information about any passage of music!

Sounds
To get the most from this book, you will need a multi-FX unit or a few individual pedals.

Unless otherwise indicated, a straightforward clean sound will work well. Specific sound indications include the following:

W/ DIST. **Distortion.** This is generally associated with the rock pieces, so fairly heavy distortion or overdrive is appropriate.

W/ CRUNCH **Crunch.** Slight distortion or overdrive.

W/ CHORUS **Chorus, etc.** Modulation effects (chorus, flanging, etc.) are generally interchangeable in this book.

W/ WAH **Wah-Wah.** If you do not have a wah pedal, you can use auto-wah or heavy phasing or flanging.

Notation types
Each piece uses one or more of the following types of notation:

Lead/single notes
Play the notes musically in the given rhythm and style; matters of phrasing and articulation are generally up to you (see "Signs and Symbols").

Chords notated as notes

This example uses power chords (root and fifth), but more complex chords are sometimes written out when a specific voicing is required. All but the cruelest of arrangers generally add chord symbols—if you can't work out the exact voicing in time, at least you will be playing the right chord.

Chords notated as slashes

Here the chords are written as symbols; the voicing is up to you and is dictated by the style of the piece. Play the chords in the rhythm shown.

Chord chart with non-specific rhythm

Both the voicings and exact rhythm are up to you in this situation; again, decide what is required based on the style of the piece.

Signs and symbols

Slurs

These are generally best interpreted as hammer-ons and pull-offs, but slides and bends could be appropriate too. Specific slides are often indicated with a short line between notes, as in the second measure below.

Accents and articulations

ACCENT   SHARP   STACCATO   MUTE   HARMONIC
ACCENT   (SHORT)

Other instructions

P.M.-------- ⊣   CONT. SIM. AD LIB.

CONT. SIM.   Continue in a similar way.

P.M.   Palm mute.

AD LIB.   At will.

Bis (repeat) Bars

Repeat the previous bar.

2
Repeat the previous two bars.

4
Repeat the previous four bars.

A word about tuning

"What's with this guy? I know how to tune a guitar. Give me a break!"

OK, maybe you do. But, to my ears at least, a lot of players sound *very nearly but not quite* in tune. The difference may be tiny, but it does make a big difference.

Of course, occasionally there just isn't time. If you're playing a one-hour party set with little or no break between songs, you just have to "wing it." In this situation it helps to have a guitar that holds its tuning, and a good stage tuner.

If you're tuning by ear (and I often find that electronic tuners don't *quite* get there), there are several methods to choose from but, oddly enough, the one we all learn first is actually the best:

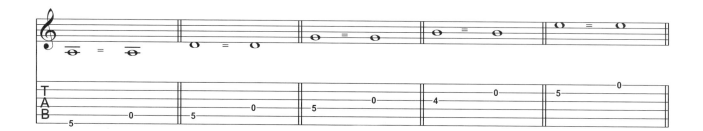

After this basic tuning, check the following octaves:

- high E string, 7th fret against open B string—adjust B string
- high E string, 3rd fret against open G string—adjust G string
- B string, 3rd fret against open D string—adjust D string

- G string, 2nd fret against open A string—adjust A string
- D string, 2nd fret against open E string—adjust E string

Finally, check the top and bottom E strings. If they don't sound perfectly in tune, go back to the top of this procedure until you find the error.

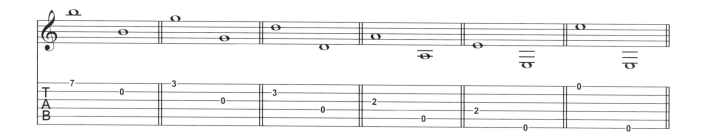

Don't be tempted to use harmonics. The modern guitar has to be tuned to *equal temperament*. Harmonics produce mathematically *pure* intervals, which actually sound better in their own right, but are unfortunately incompatible with the guitar's fret spacing.

For now, tune your guitar (from low to high) to **Track 1** on the accompanying CD.

CD track 2

CD track 3

W/ DIST.

CONT. SIM. W/FILLS

CD track 4

CD track 5

W/ SLIGHT CRUNCH

CD track 6

CD track 7

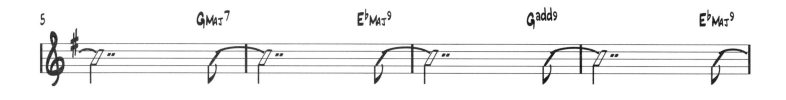

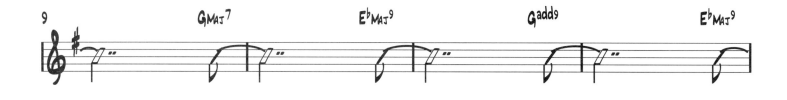

CD track 8

CD track 9

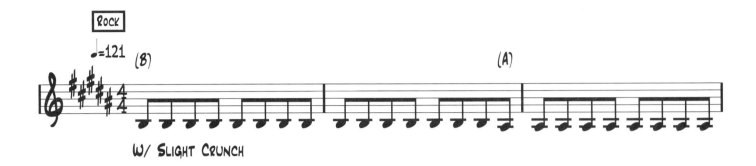

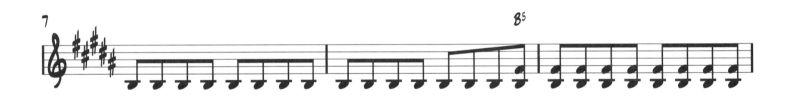

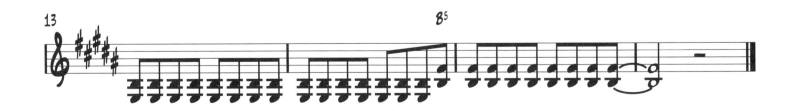

CD track 10

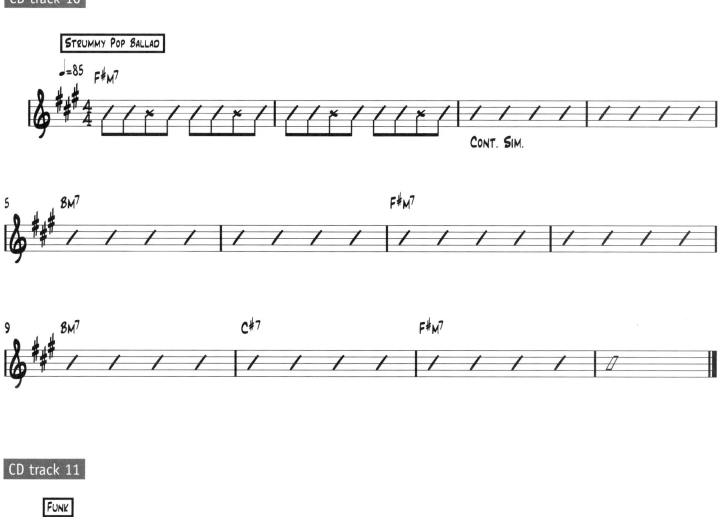

CD track 11

CD track 12

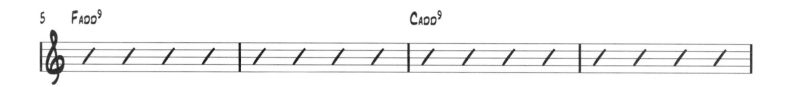

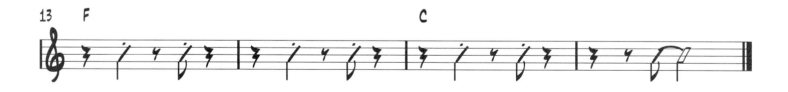

CD track 13

CD track 14

CD track 15

CD track 16

CD track 17

Disco

♩=110

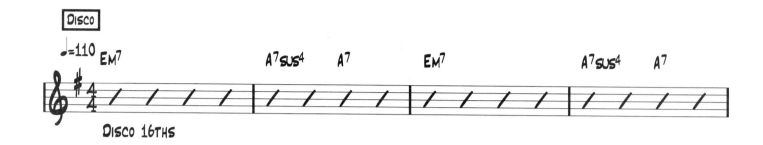

5

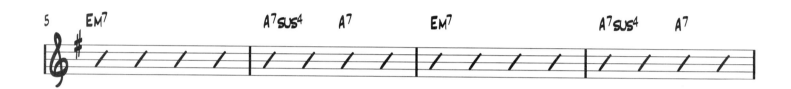

9

12

15

CD track 18

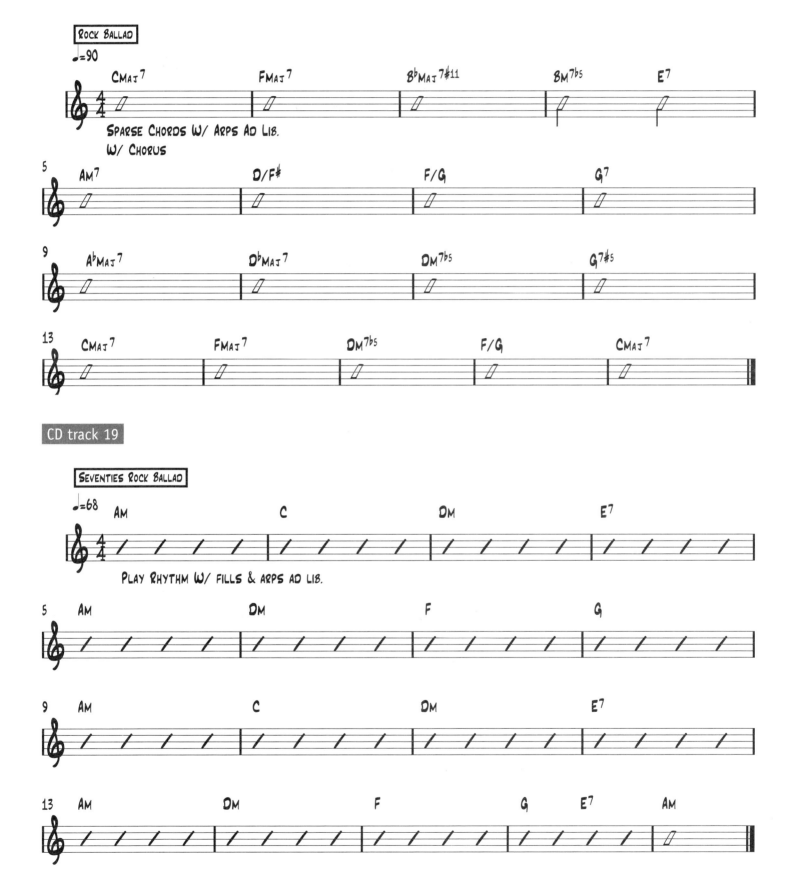

CD track 20

CD track 21

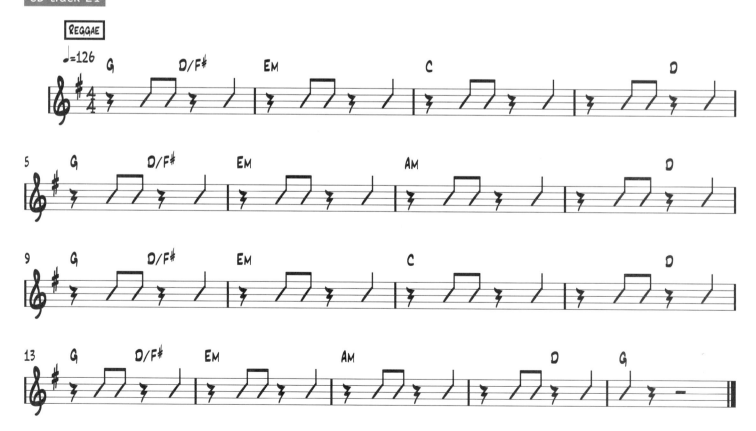

CD track 22

ROCK 'N' ROLL FILLS

W/SLIGHT CRUNCH

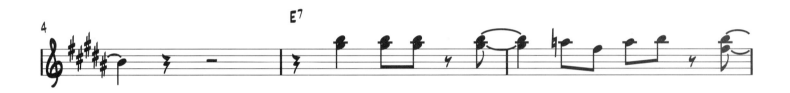

CD track 23

CD track 24

CD track 25

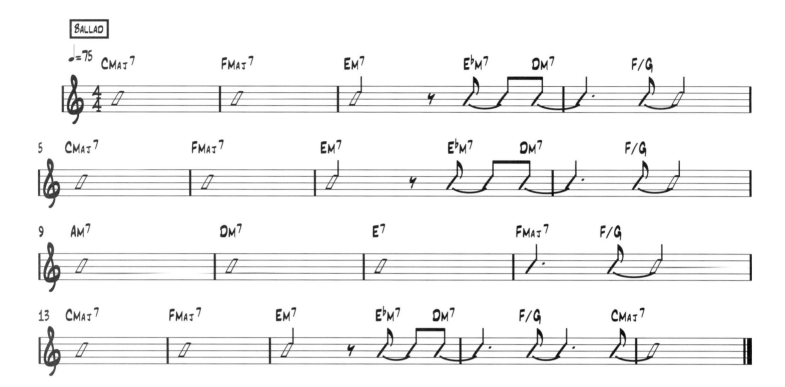

CD track 26

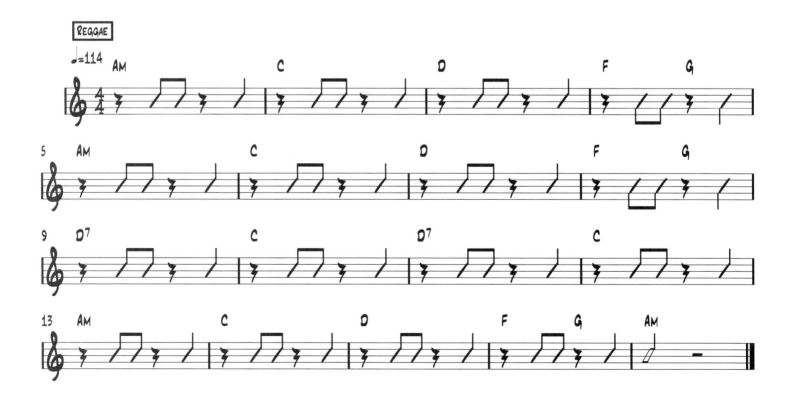

CD track 27

CD track 28

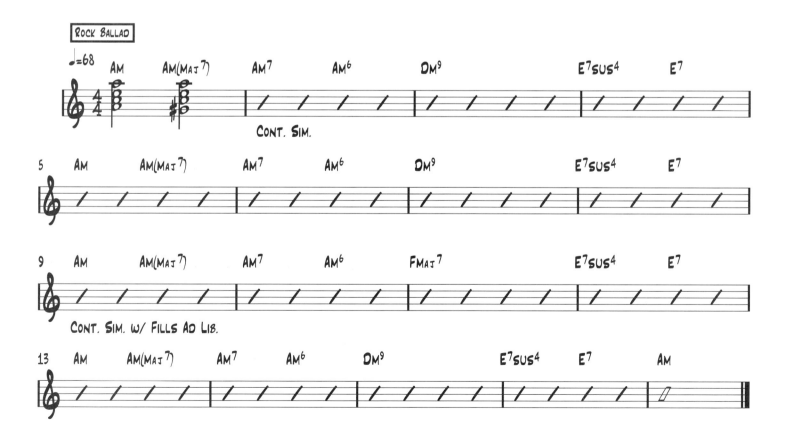

CD track 29

CD track 30

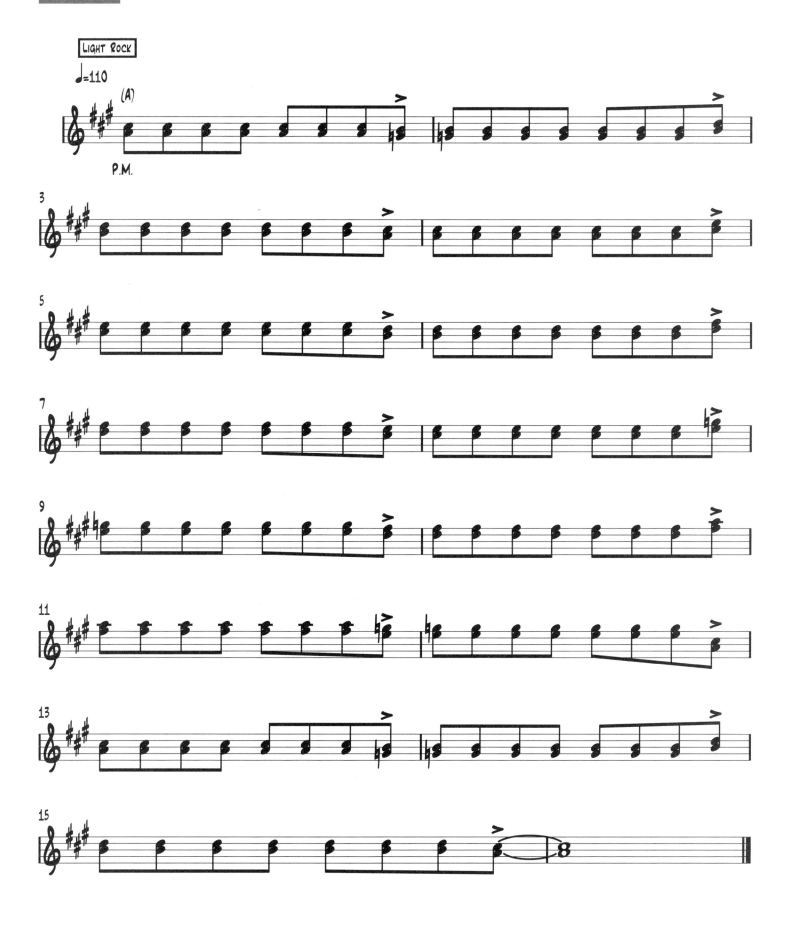

CD track 31

HEAVY ROCK

CD track 32

NEO-CLASSICAL ROCK

♩=140

W/ HEAVY DIST.

CD track 33

CD track 34

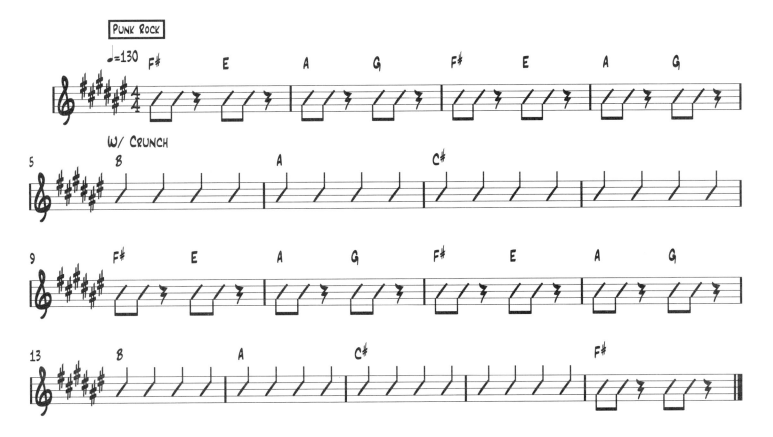

CD track 35

CD track 36

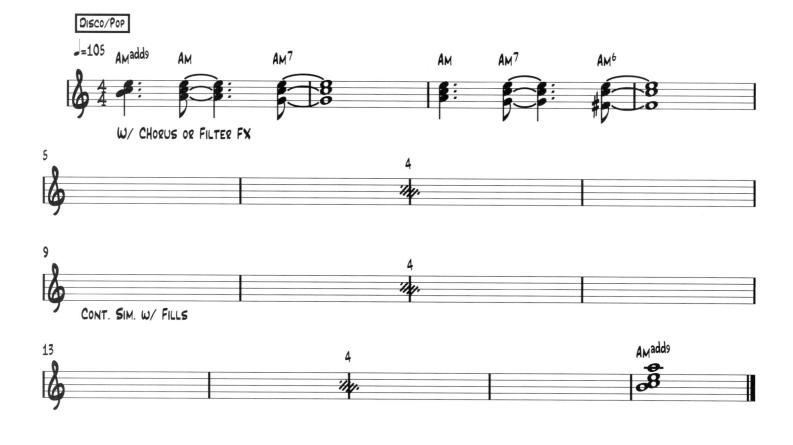

CD track 37

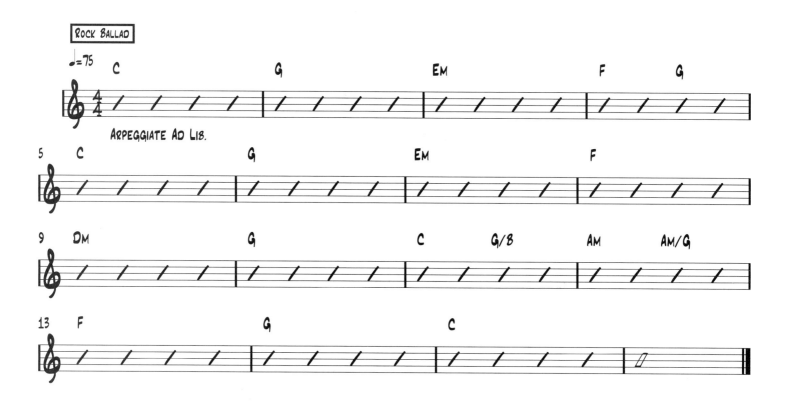

CD track 38

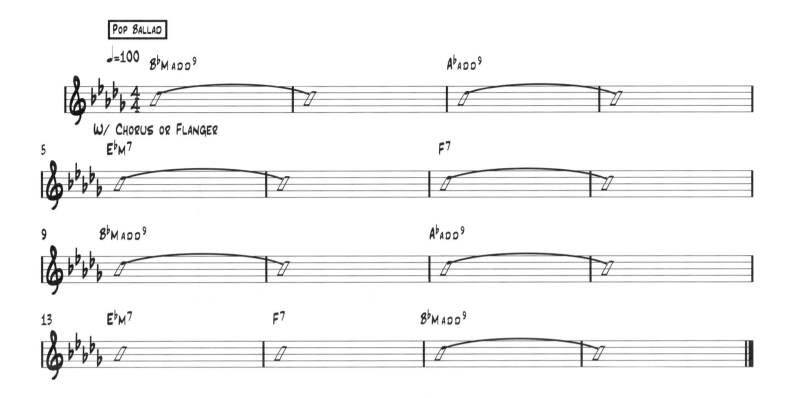

CD track 39

CD track 40

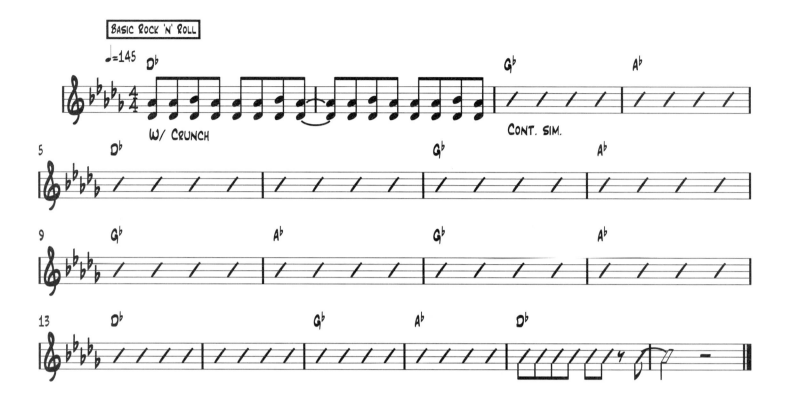

CD track 41

CD track 42

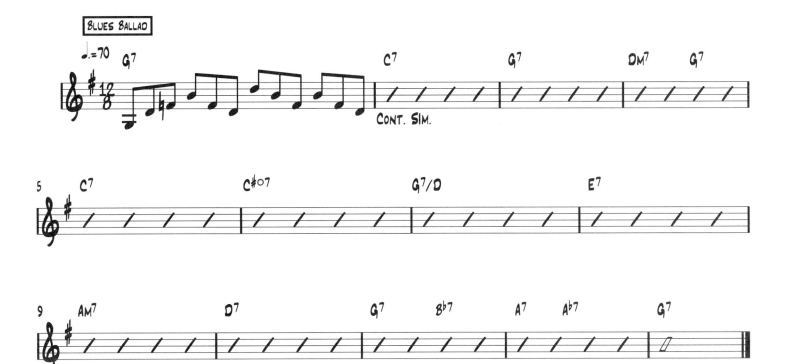

CD track 43

CD track 44

CD track 45

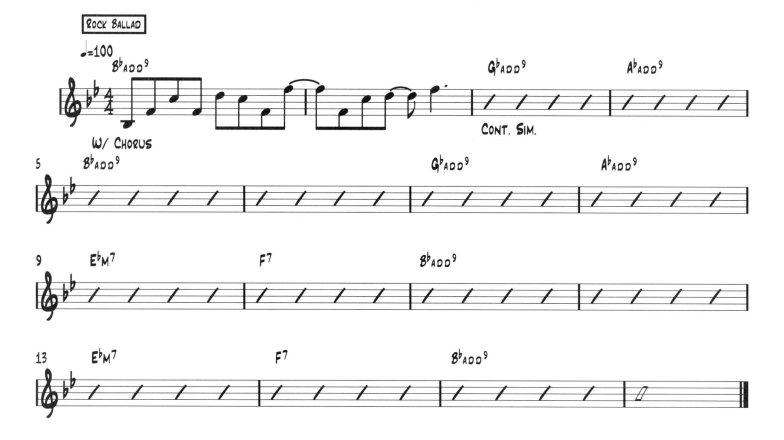

CD track 46

CD track 47

CD track 48

CD track 49

FUNKY TV THEME

W/ SLIGHT DIST.

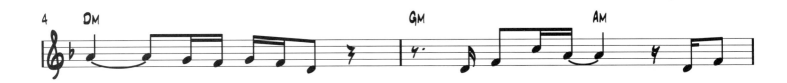

CD track 50

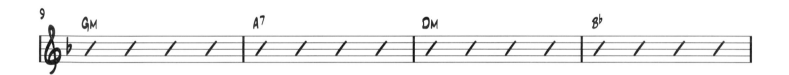

Appleby, Amy. *Start Reading Music.* New York: Amsco 1992. A proven method to mastering sightreading basics. Whether you are an instrumentalist, singer, or composer, you can take a giant leap forward by learning to read music.

Appleby, Amy, and Peter Pickow. *The Guitarist's Handbook.* New York: Amsco 2002. Five guitar reference books in one handy volume: Guitar Owner's Manual, Music Theory For Guitarists, Guitar Scale Dictionary, Guitar Chord Dictionary, and Guitar Manuscript Paper. For both acoustic and electric guitarists.

The Complete Guitar Player Songbook, Omnibus Edition 2. New York: Amsco 2004. This compilation of three NEW Complete Guitar Player songbooks contains over 100 songs written by such great songwriters as Bob Dylan, Paul Simon, Elton John, Cat Stevens, John Denver, and many others. Full lyrics are given for each song.

Dineen, Joe, and Mark Bridges. *The Gig Bag Book Of Guitar Complete.* New York: Amsco 2001. A sampler of The Gig Bag Book Of Scales, Arpeggios, and Tab Chords. Each two-page spread illustrates a scale with corresponding arpeggio and chords.

Every Musician's Handbook. New York: Amsco 1984. This pocket-sized resource covers rules of harmony, counterpoint, and orchestration. With sections on scales, keys, and chords, plus a musical term glossary.

Lozano, Ed. *Easy Blues Songbook.* New York: Amsco 1997. Learn the art of blues playing by jamming along to the actual tunes made famous by authentic blues artists. Fourteen tunes arranged for easy guitar with note-for-note transcriptions in standard notation and tablature.

Lozano, Ed, and Joe Dineen. *Mastering Modes For Guitar.* New York: Amsco 2002. This practical guide unlocks the mystery behind the construction and application of over 60 modes. Includes special sections on advanced and world scales. All of the examples are demonstrated on the accompanying CD.

Salvador, Sal. *Single String Studies For Guitar.* Miami: Belwin 1966. Simply the best book for alternate picking. A complete study of single string exercises designed to build technique and control.

Scharfglass, Matt. *The Gig Bag Book Of Practical Pentatonics For All Guitarists.* New York: Amsco 2000. The ultimate compact reference book of pentatonic scales (five-note minor and major scales) and how to use them. Packed with over 400 riffs and examples; also includes a section on theory and more.

Scharfglass, Matt. *You Can Do It: Play Guitar Dammit!* New York: Amsco 2004. This proven method will have you spinning off chords, riffs, and solos in as little time as possible. Includes a specially designed CD with demonstrations of all the music examples plus additional backup tracks.

Willard, Jerry, editor and arranger. *Fifty Easy Classical Guitar Pieces.* New York: Amsco 2004. Contains a delightful repertory of pieces for the beginning or intermediate player, drawn from all periods of classical guitar literature. Includes a full-length CD of all the pieces performed by the author. Learn pieces by Sor, Carulli, Giuliani, Dowland, Bach, DeVisee, and many more.